# Hello School!

# School!

## Full of Poems

### by Dee Lillegard

### illustrated by Don Carter

Dell Dragonfly Books New York

**School**
Wakes up early.
Just can't wait
to see who's coming.
*Don't be late!*

### New Shoes

They stand at the door,
too shy to walk.
They have tongues,
but they don't talk . . .

## Cubbies
Sad when empty
When filled,
thrilled!

AMY

JACK

## Hook
*Hurry!*
If you give him a minute,
he'll grab your jacket
... with *you* in it!

**Teacher's Desk**
Impressively large.
*She's* in charge!

## Pencil

Wiggles and squiggles a scary face.
Then flips himself over—
*Erase! Erase!*

## Paper

What's he hiding?
What's he about?
He needs your hand
to draw him out . . .

## Crayon

Starts out tall
with a fine pointed head.
Never grows up . . .
grows *down* instead.

## Scissors

*Open shut*
*Open shut*
A snippy pair,
they're quick to cut.

## Glue

*Stick with me,*
says Glue with a grin,
*and I'll stick with you . . .*
*through thick and thin.*

## Letters

They stand in line from A to Z,
longing to be wild and free,
to fly away like breezy birds . . .
in flocks of *words!*

## Wastebasket

*Feed me, feed me!*
*Yum yum yum . . .*
*Toss your tidbits*
*into my tum!*

## Calendar

January, February, March . . .
Monday, Tuesday, too.
Months and days of the week
he'll proudly display for you.

## Swings

They hang around,
stare at the sky . . .
wait to be sat on
so they can *fly!*

## Fence

Stands guard . . . all day.
Wishes he could run and play.
Loves it when kids come his way.

## Slide

Slippery slithery
Slide says, *Go!*
*This is no time to be shy*
*or slow.*

**Rug**

Likes nothing more
than snoozing
on the floor.
Listen closely.
Hear him snore?

## Clock

Watches all the time.
Worries, *Am I late?*
Always on the move.
Impatient. Won't wait.

## Books

Closed shut . . .
Secrets to hide?
Or waiting for you to say
*Open wide!*

## Fountain

Gushes and bubbles
when you turn her on.
Hangs her head quietly
after you're gone.

## Window

Shows us if it's sunny,
or if the weather's drippy-runny,
or if the clouds are acting *funny* . . .

## Numbers

1's a stick.
2's a birdie.
3 is bubbly.
4 is sturdy.
If fidgety 5
gets out of line,
down go 6,
7, 8, 9!

## Paintbrush

When paint gets in his hair,
Brush creates a scene,
swishing yellow, swashing red,
splashing blue and green.

## Table

Loves a mess.
Oh yes!

## Clay

A squooshy mooshy
shape-changer.
Pick her up
and re-arrange her!

## Easel

Easily stands for hours,
holding up *mountains* . . .
or flowers.

## Chair

Doesn't mind
your behind.
Prefers your seat
to shoes or feet.

## Beads

Scattery chattery,
wondering whether
they want to be strung
on a string all together.

## Blocks

They mumble, fumble,
climb from their jumble.
Up they scramble!
Then grumble when they
tumble . . .

## Truck

*Vroom! Vroom!*
*Across the room . . .*
*Look out, feet.*
*Here I zoom!*

## Puzzle

Falls to pieces . . .
gets mixed up that way.
Hopes you will put him
together today.

## Puppet

Give me your hand; your voice, too.
Then see what a hollow-head fellow
can do . . .

## Costume Box

Opens up and spills out
capes, scarves, a pig's snout,
a clown's nose and floppy feet,
witch's wand and ghostly sheet,
wigs and hats of every hue . . .
*Get ready to be someone new!*

## Drum

*Rum-tum! Rum-tum!*
*Bang-a-bang-a-bam!*
*A happy-to-be-noisy person . . .*
*that's what I am!*

## Xylophone

*Hammer me. It's okay.*
*It's my favorite way to play.*

## Tambourine

*Shake-a-shake-a-shake!*
*I love the sound I make!*

**Door**
Opens wide
to let us know
it's time to go.

**Bye-bye, School!**

A smile.
A sigh.
School waves
*Bye-bye . . .*

For the Bryants,
Charles and Debra, Chaz
and Eli—and their
California cousins.

—D.L.

To my heroes:
Maurice Sendak, Tomie
dePaola, Dan Yaccarino,
Lane Smith, William Joyce,
and Curious George.

—D.C.

Published by
Dell Dragonfly Books
an imprint of
Random House Children's Books
a division of Random House, Inc.
1540 Broadway
New York, New York 10036
Text copyright © 2001 by Dee Lillegard
Illustrations copyright © 2001 by Donald J. Carter

Visit us on the Web! www.randomhouse.com/kids
Educators and librarians, for a variety of teaching tools, visit us at www.randomhouse.com/teachers
Library of Congress Cataloging-in-Publication Data
Lillegard, Dee.
Hello school! : a classroom full of poems / by Dee Lillegard ; illustrated by Don Carter.
p. cm.
ISBN: 0-375-81020-X (trade)
0-375-91020-4 (lib. bdg.)
0-440-41777-5 (pbk.)
1. Education, Preschool—Juvenile poetry. 2. Kindergarten—Juvenile poetry. 3. Schools—Juvenile poetry. 4. Children's
poetry, American. [1. Kindergarten—Poetry. 2. Schools—Poetry. 3. American poetry.]    I. Carter, Don, 1958– ill. II. Title.
PS3562.I4557 H45 2001
811'.54—dc21
00-059923
Reprinted by arrangement with Alfred A. Knopf
Printed in the United States of America
July 2003
10 9 8 7 6 5 4 3 2 1